Boxing's
HEAVYWEIGHT
CHAMPIONS

Boxing's
HEAVYWEIGHT
CHAMPIONS

Richard Rainbolt

 Lerner Publications Company
Minneapolis

ACKNOWLEDGMENTS

The illustrations are reproduced through the courtesy of: pp. 6, 9, 11, 22, 25, 34, 40, 42, 45, 47, 51, 57, 58, 60, 64, 67, United Press International; p. 14, Library of Congress; pp. 17, 21, 26, 29, 54, 69, 71, Wide World Photos; p. 31, *The Ring Magazine*; p. 36, Independent Picture Service.

LIBRARY OF CONGRESS CATALOGING IN PUBLICATION DATA

Rainbolt, Richard.
  Boxing's heavyweight champions.

  (The Sports Heroes Library)
  SUMMARY: Biographies of ten heavyweight prize fighters:
John L. Sullivan, Jim Corbett, Robert Fitzsimmons, Jim Jeffries,
Jack Johnson, Jack Dempsey, Gene Tunney, Joe Louis, Rocky
Marciano, and Muhammad Ali.

  1. Boxing—Biography—Juvenile literature. [1. Boxing—
Biography] I. Title.

GV1131.R34 1975   796.8'3'0922[B][920]   74-27470
ISBN 0-8225-1053-7

Published simultaneously in Canada by
J. M. Dent & Sons (Canada) Ltd., Don Mills, Ontario

Manufactured in the United States of America

International Standard Book Number: 0-8225-1053-7
Library of Congress Catalog Card Number: 74-27470

Contents

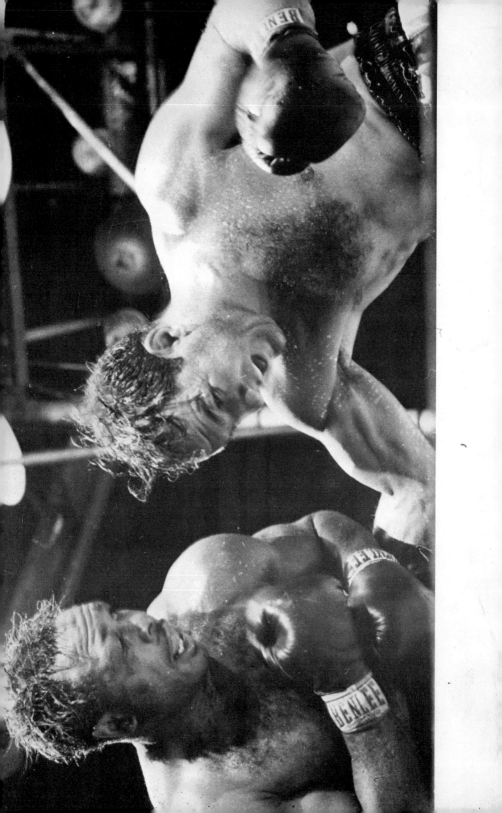

Introduction

Who is the greatest heavyweight champion of all time? The answer depends on whom you ask. There are as many different answers as there are heavyweight champions. You probably will have your own opinion after reading the life stories of 10 great champions in this book.

These 10 champions held their titles at different times over the last 100 years. But the history of boxing goes back further than this. Boxing tournaments were held during the Olympic Games in Greece as far back as 688 B.C. The modern form of boxing began in England in the early 1700s. That also was when the first boxing rules were set down. These rules made it illegal to hit a man below the belt or while he was down.

Since the British boxers did not wear gloves, their fights came to be called "bare-knuckle" matches. Each round lasted until one of the opponents was knocked down. The match lasted until one of the opponents could not come back from a knockdown. Bare-knuckle matches were very brutal, and sometimes fighters died in the ring.

Boxing first became popular in the United States in the early 1800s. But gamblers and criminals soon took control of the sport. They bribed boxers to fix title fights. Many people disapproved of boxing because they believed that it was just a sport for criminals. People also disapproved of the sport because the bare-knuckle fights were so brutal. As a result, laws against boxing were passed in many parts of the country.

In the late 1800s, boxing became popular again in the United States, even though it was still illegal. The reason for this new interest in boxing was John L. Sullivan, America's first real sports hero. Sullivan traveled around the country, taking part in exhibition matches. These were matches in which boxers sparred, or hit each other lightly, while wearing gloves. Unlike title matches, they did not last until a boxer suffered a knockout or took such a beating that he couldn't stand up. Also, since the boxers wore gloves, there were not many serious injuries. The police allowed these matches because they were more like stage shows than fights. Bare-knuckle title matches were held too. But these bouts were fought in secret so that the police could not break them up.

In the early 1900s, boxing became legal in many states. Even in those states where it was still illegal, the police often allowed title matches to be held in private clubs or gyms. During these years bare-knuckle fighting became a thing of the past. All matches were fought with gloves. More important, new rules were set up that made the sport less brutal. Rounds were limited to three minutes, and the fighters had a one-minute rest between rounds.

From the beginning of the sport, there have always been different weight divisions in boxing. But the matches fought by heavyweights have usually been the most popular. A heavyweight fighter usually weighs about 175 pounds or more. Unlike the other divisions, there is no limit on how much a heavyweight fighter can weigh. Because of their size, the heavyweights are the most powerful boxers in the ring. Many people think that heavyweight bouts are the most exciting to watch because they are hard-hitting fights that often end in knockouts.

Here are the stories of 10 of these powerful heavyweights. Some were probably better boxers than the others. Some had tough fights and others had easy fights before and during their championship years. But each contributed in his own way to the history of heavyweight boxing.

John L. Sullivan meets Jack Kilrain for a heavyweight bout in 1889.

John L. Sullivan

No other heavyweight champion ever fought as many bouts as John L. Sullivan, the "Boston Strong Boy." Sullivan fought over 200 matches—about 100 more fights than any other heavyweight champ in the history of boxing.

John Lawrence Sullivan was born in Boston, Massachusetts, in 1858. Sullivan was a good athlete as a boy, and baseball was his favorite sport. Because his family was poor, John L. had to quit high school and go to work. He worked as a brick carrier, like his father. But this job ended quickly when Sullivan broke his boss's nose in a fight.

Sullivan then began spending his time at boxing exhibitions. Once when Sullivan was at an exhibition, a boxer said that he would spar with any person in the audience. Sullivan took the offer and got into the ring. Even though he had never boxed with gloves before, Sullivan knocked the fighter out of the ring. After that, Sullivan began to make money by sparring in boxing exhibitions. He soon became famous as the "Boston Strong Boy," and he went on a boxing tour around the country.

Sullivan's first title fight, or prizefight, was in 1881 against John Flood, a New York gangster. Because prizefighting was illegal, the men met secretly on a barge in the Hudson River. It was a bare-knuckle match, and Sullivan won by a knockout in eight rounds. This win got him a match with the U.S. heavyweight champion, Paddy Ryan. The Ryan-Sullivan match was held in Mississippi in 1882. Sullivan was an easy winner. He knocked Ryan cold in the ninth round. In fact, Sullivan threw so many hard punches that people feared he would kill Ryan.

Sullivan then went on another boxing tour around the country. He offered a $1,000 prize to anyone who could last four rounds with him. Only one man was able to do this. Altogether, Sullivan knocked out 59 men on that tour.

Sullivan's next prizefight was against Charley Mitchell, a British heavyweight boxer. This match was set up by Richard K. Fox, a U.S. magazine editor who disliked Sullivan. Fox thought John L. was a show-off, and he wanted to see him beaten. It looked like Fox might get his wish when Mitchell knocked down Sullivan in the first round. But Sullivan came back to give Mitchell such a bad beating that the police were called to stop the fight.

In 1887 the Boston Strong Boy went to England. Great crowds turned out to cheer him as a hero. Sullivan wanted to fight the two best British boxers, Charley Mitchell and Jem Smith. Sullivan did not

get a fight with Smith, but he did get a second
bout with Mitchell. The Mitchell-Sullivan match
was held in France. Heavy rain fell before and
during the bout, which was fought outdoors in a
farmyard. Sullivan did not move well in the deep
mud, and he could not knock Mitchell out. But
he did knock the British fighter down 15 times.

The two men fought for more than three hours. Finally, the fight was stopped after 39 rounds. It was called a draw.

After the Mitchell-Sullivan match, Richard Fox, the magazine editor, made a surprising announcement. He said that a boxer named Jake Kilrain was the new U.S. heavyweight champion. Fox claimed that Sullivan had lost his title because of the draw with Mitchell.

A title fight was then held between Sullivan and Kilrain in Mississippi in 1889. People all over the country became interested in the Kilrain-Sullivan match. Prizefighting was still illegal in the United States, but stories about the fight were in all the newspapers. The site of the fight was kept secret, though, so that the police would not break it up.

Sullivan weighed in at 205 pounds for the fight. He stood 5 feet, 10-1/2 inches tall. Kilrain was the same height as Sullivan, but he was 10 pounds lighter. The fight went 75 rounds before Kilrain's corner threw in the towel. Sullivan had proved again that he was the champion. This match turned out to be Sullivan's last bare-knuckle fight. It was also the last bare-knuckle championship match ever held in the United States.

After this match with Kilrain, Sullivan toured the United States and Canada as the leading actor in a stage play. He did not fight for three years, even though many boxers wanted to battle him for the title. Soon people began to demand that Sullivan get off the stage and back into the ring.

Sullivan finally agreed to fight Jim Corbett in a title match in 1892. The two men had met a year before in an exhibition match during which they had only sparred. Corbett was a young fighter who relied on speed and skill in the ring. This kind of boxing was new to Sullivan. He believed a strong punch was the only way to win a fight.

When the two men weighed in, John L. was 34 pounds heavier than Corbett. Because of his lighter weight, Corbett was able to move faster than Sullivan in the ring. He danced out of the way of Sullivan's punches until the champion grew tired. Then Corbett moved in and started to hit Sullivan. He finally knocked out the Boston Strong Boy in the 21st round.

The Corbett-Sullivan match was fought under new rules that included the use of boxing gloves. This new style of fighting was not for John L. He liked to fight chin-to-chin with bare knuckles. After he lost to Corbett, Sullivan quit boxing. He appeared in stage plays for a while and remained very popular. Eventually he retired to a farm in Massachusetts, where he died in 1918.

Jim Corbett

Jim Corbett changed the sport of boxing. Corbett proved that strength alone was not always enough to win bouts. With his defeat of the powerful John L. Sullivan in 1892, Corbett showed how important speed and skill were in the ring.

Jim Corbett was born in San Francisco, California, in 1866. His father wanted him to be a priest. But young Jim had other ideas. He dreamed of being a baseball player like his older brother. As it turned out, Corbett did neither of these things. Instead, from the time he was 17 years old, he devoted his life to boxing.

Corbett learned how to box at a boys' club, and he learned fast. In fact, he looked so good in the ring that he was matched against the club's middleweight champion. Corbett knocked the champ through the ropes and won the fight easily. He then went on to become heavyweight champion of the club. Before long, the young fighter became known as a great amateur boxer all along the West Coast. Corbett took the sport very seriously. He practiced every day and always looked for new ways to improve his skill in the ring. When professional fighters came through San Francisco, he asked if he could spar with them.

Corbett turned professional in 1889. Boxing fans began to call him "Gentleman Jim" because of his good looks, fancy clothes, and polite manners. Corbett may have been a gentleman outside of the ring, but in the ring he was a tough fighter.

Jim Corbett gained national fame in 1890 after a fight with Jake Kilrain. Kilrain had fought a good bout against John L. Sullivan only a short time before, and he was favored to beat Gentleman Jim. But instead, Corbett defeated Kilrain in only 6 rounds. Corbett then went on to meet Peter Jackson, the top Australian boxer. Again, everyone thought that Corbett would lose. The match went 61 rounds and lasted more than four hours. To everyone's surprise, it ended in a draw.

A year after the Jackson-Corbett match, John L. Sullivan agreed to meet Gentleman Jim for a heavyweight title bout. Once more, everyone thought that Corbett would lose. And again, Corbett proved them wrong. He knocked out Sullivan in the 21st round.

At first, the new champion was not well liked by boxing fans. John L. Sullivan had been a popular champion, and many people resented Corbett for beating him. But Corbett became better liked after he toured the country in a stage play called *Gentleman Jack*. He was a skilled actor, and people were impressed by his good looks and manners.

More than a year passed before Corbett boxed

again. A match was finally set up between Corbett and Charley Mitchell, the British heavyweight champion. The fight was held in 1894, and Corbett knocked out Mitchell in the third round. By defeating the Englishman, Corbett became America's first *world* heavyweight champion.

Corbett fought his next heavyweight title fight three years later. His opponent was "Ruby Robert" Fitzsimmons. The Corbett-Fitzsimmons match was one of the most colorful in the history of boxing. A huge crowd came to the bout, which was held on St. Patrick's Day in 1897 in Carson City, Nevada. It was the first title match to be filmed. Also, it was the first match where a woman sat in a fighter's corner. Mrs. Robert Fitzsimmons was that woman. There was a special guest in Corbett's corner, too— Wyatt Earp, the famous western sheriff. And another well-known sheriff, Bat Masterson, collected the fans' guns before the fight.

Fitzsimmons weighed only 156 pounds, compared to Corbett's 178 pounds. But Ruby Robert was a smart fighter with a strong punch. At first, it looked like it was Corbett's match all the way, especially when he knocked down Ruby Robert in the 6th round. But Fitzsimmons got up and kept going. In the 14th round, Fitz claimed the title with a left to Corbett's stomach and jaw.

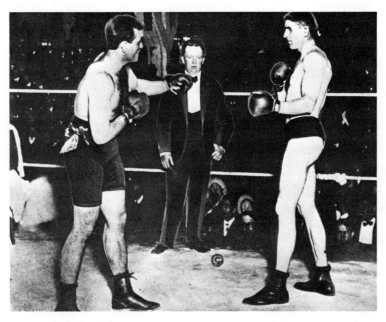

The Corbett-Jeffries match, 1900

In 1900, Corbett tried to regain the title in a match with the new heavyweight champion, Jim Jeffries. Corbett was still fast, and his quick jabs hit Jeffries's face round after round. But in the 20th round, Gentleman Jim began to tire. Jeffries then started to land his powerful punches. A solid right to the jaw knocked Corbett out in the 23rd round.

Three years later, Corbett tried another comeback against Jeffries. This time Jeffries won by a knockout in the 10th round. After this defeat, Corbett retired from the ring and took up acting again. Gentleman Jim Corbett died in 1933.

Robert Fitzsimmons

Robert Fitzsimmons was the lightest heavy-weight champion in the history of boxing. When he took the title from Gentleman Jim Corbett, Fitz weighed only 156 pounds. Fitzsimmons was also the only champion ever to win titles in three weight divisions—middleweight, light-heavyweight, and heavyweight.

Robert Fitzsimmons was born in England in 1862. His family moved to New Zealand when he was nine years old. There he went to school for only a short time before he began working as a blacksmith's helper. It was this kind of heavy work that gave Fitzsimmons his strong shoulders and chest.

When he was 18 years old, Fitz fought in his first boxing tournament. At that time, he weighed only 140 pounds. But his strong muscles made up for his light weight. He knocked out four opponents in one night at the tournament. As a result, he became the amateur heavyweight champion of New Zealand.

Fitzsimmons then went to Australia, where he took all of his opponents. In 1890, when he was 28 years old, he sailed for California to look for new matches. At first, the boxing crowd in San Francisco did not believe that the skinny Fitz was a heavyweight fighter. They matched him against a top middleweight boxer. Fitzsimmons hit his opponent so hard that the man went flying across the ring.

In 1891, Fitzsimmons won the middleweight championship of the United States. After taking that title, Fitzsimmons became known throughout the country. Boxing fans began to call him "Ruby Robert" because of his bright red hair and freckled face.

When he was 35 years old, Fitz got the chance to meet Jim Corbett for the world heavyweight title. After defeating Corbett in a 14-round battle, Fitzsimmons said that he would never fight again. He then took up acting for a while. But he didn't stay out of the ring for long. He began fighting again and went on to add the world light-heavyweight championship to his list of titles.

When Ruby Robert was 40 years old, he met Jim Jeffries for a heavyweight championship title match in 1899. Jeffries was only 27 years old, and he outweighed Fitz by 50 pounds. The fight went 11 rounds, with Fitz unable to land a good punch. Jeffries finally knocked out the champ with a short left to his chin. Three years later, the two met again. This time Fitzsimmons had the best of Jeffries in the early rounds. But the bigger and younger Jeffries won by a knockout in the 6th round.

In 1894, Ruby Robert Fitzsimmons (left) took the heavyweight title from Jim Corbett.

Fitzsimmons didn't quit boxing until 1914, when he was 52 years old. The records show that he had 65 fights during his career, but he probably fought more than 100 in all. He died in Chicago in 1917.

Jim Jeffries

Many boxing experts say that Jim Jeffries was the hardest-hitting heavyweight to enter the ring. "Big Jeff" was so strong that he could knock out an opponent with only a short punch.

Jim Jeffries was born in Ohio in 1875. His father was a traveling preacher, and the family moved to California when Jim was still a boy. The Jeffries were poor, and Jim worked in a factory instead of going to school. By the time he was 17 years old, Jeffries was working in the California copper mines. It was there that he had his first fight. Jeffries and the biggest man in the mines started wrestling, but it soon turned into a fist fight. After almost an hour of steady battling, Jeffries was still standing. The big miner could not get up.

After this fight, Jeffries thought he might have a career in the ring. He went to Los Angeles, where he got two professional fights. The young boxer won both by knockouts in the second rounds. Jeffries then went to Carson City, Nevada. There he became a sparring partner for Jim Corbett, who was training for his title match with Bob Fitzsimmons. Big Jeff became famous only a few days after he arrived in Carson City. The newspapers ran a story that said Jeffries had knocked down Corbett during a sparring session. Corbett denied the story. Jeffries said nothing at the time, but some years later, he admitted the story was true.

After leaving Carson City, Jeffries began to fight some of the top heavyweights in the country. It was in one of these bouts that the young boxer learned a lesson that changed his style of fighting. Big Jeff often forgot to protect himself as he rushed at his opponents. But after taking a hard punch that broke his nose and several teeth, he developed the "Jeffries Crouch." He continued to rush his opponents, but he did so with his head and belly tucked in. He bent his legs in a crouch, kept his right arm close to protect his body, and swung out at his opponent with his left. The Jeffries Crouch made it very hard for anyone to seriously hurt the big fighter.

Jeffries had fought only 10 professional bouts when he met Bob Fitzsimmons for the heavyweight title in 1899. Fitz had never fought a man who used a crouch like Jeffries. The champ could not land a good punch. Jeffries took the title with a knockout in the 11th round.

The new world champion first defended his title later that same year against Tom Sharkey. After staying 25 rounds with Jeffries, Sharkey went to the hospital with three broken ribs. Jeffries then faced the man he had once sparred with—"Gentleman Jim" Corbett. Although he was not as fast as he used to be, Corbett fought one of the best matches of his career. He held Jeffries for 23 rounds before losing on a knockout.

In 1902, Jeffries had a rematch with the man he had taken the title from—Bob Fitzsimmons. "Ruby Robert" was then 43 years old, and he could not keep pace with the young champ. Jeffries knocked him out in the eighth round.

After defending his title two more times, Jeffries retired in 1905. There were no other good heavyweights around for him to fight. That same year, Jeffries refereed a fight between two heavyweights—Marvin Hart and Jack Root. After Hart

"Shake hands, and come out fighting!" Jim Jeffries (left) and Bob Fitzsimmons before their second bout in 1902

won the match, Jeffries named him the new heavy-weight champion. Many people did not think Hart had a claim to the title. They said that Big Jeff did not have the right to name a new champion, especially since he could have beaten both Hart and Root easily. But Hart went ahead and defended his doubtful title anyway. Within a year, he was defeated by Tommy Burns. Burns then lost to Jack Johnson, who became the first black heavyweight champion.

After Johnson took the title, Jeffries came out of retirement to fight him. Johnson and Jeffries met in Reno, Nevada, in 1910. It had been five years since Big Jeff's last bout. He was 35 years old and overweight. Right from the beginning, it was plain that Jeffries would lose the match. Johnson knocked out the old champ in the 15th round, after giving him a hard beating.

That was Jeffries's last fight. He then retired for good to his California farm, where he died in 1952.

Jack Johnson

Today some boxing experts call Jack Johnson the greatest heavyweight of all time. But while Johnson was fighting, most people refused to give him any credit for his skill in the ring. Johnson had to wait nine years before he was given a chance at the heavyweight title. During those years, he fought almost 100 bouts—more bouts than most of the heavyweight champs had in their whole careers.

John Arthur Johnson was born in Galveston, Texas, in 1878. As a child, he was nicknamed "Little Arthur" because he was so small. Sportswriters later called Johnson by this name, even though it no longer fit him. Little Arthur grew to be over 6 feet tall and to weigh 205 pounds.

Johnson began boxing as a teenager when he worked in a gym. He liked the sport so much that he used to carry boxing gloves around and look for fights on street corners. To get more experience, Johnson left Galveston and started hanging around gyms in Chicago, New York, and Boston. Soon he was sparring with professional fighters. At the beginning of his professional career, Johnson suffered two knockouts. But he learned from his mistakes and went on to become a winner in the ring.

Johnson tried to get a fight with Tommy Burns, the world heavyweight champion, for many years.

Burns always talked about how much better he was than Johnson, but he would not meet Johnson in the ring to prove it. The two finally met for the title in Sidney, Australia, in 1908. Johnson made no mistakes. He outboxed the champion right from the beginning and could have won the bout by a knockout in any round. But instead he made Burns suffer through a 14-round beating. Jackson wanted to punish Burns for making him wait so long for a title match. The one-sided battle was finally stopped by the police. Johnson was given the decision, and he became the first black heavyweight champion.

Johnson's second title bout came a year later in California. This one was against Stanley Ketchell, the middleweight champion. Ketchell stood just 5 feet, 9 inches tall, and he weighed only 170 pounds. Johnson outweighed the middleweight by some 40 pounds. But Ketchell had a powerful punch to go with his dream of beating the heavyweight champ. In the first 11 rounds, neither boxer landed any hard blows. But in the 12th, Ketchell banged Johnson below the ear and dropped him. When the champ got up, Ketchell rushed at him with arms swinging. But Johnson was ready for him. He put all his weight and strength into a right uppercut that hit Ketchell full in the mouth.

Jack Johnson waits while ex-champ Jim Jeffries tries to get back on his feet.

Ketchell did not wake up for an hour. All of his front teeth were knocked out by the blow.

Johnson seemed to be unbeatable. Some boxing people who disliked him began searching for a fighter who could end Little Arthur's winning streak. Finally, they talked Jim Jeffries, the retired champion, into meeting Johnson. The Johnson-Jeffries bout was held in 1910 in Reno, Nevada. There were 20,000 people at the match. Some had traveled from as far away as Europe and Australia. All the old champions came to cheer on Jeffries—Sullivan, Corbett, Fitzsimmons, and Burns.

The ex-champion had not fought for five years,

34

and he was out of shape. Johnson pounded Jeffries for 14 rounds. In the 15th round, he knocked Jeffries down three times. That was when Jeffries's corner threw in the towel. After the fight, Jeffries said that even in his best years, he never could have beaten Johnson.

About three years after this match, Johnson got into trouble with the law. He left the United States to avoid going to jail. For seven years, Johnson traveled around Europe, meeting with anyone who wanted a match. Then, in 1915, he was offered $30,000 to defend his title. Johnson was out of money, and he took the match.

Johnson's opponent was the giant Jess Willard, who stood 6 feet, 6 inches tall and weighed 250 pounds. Twenty-thousand fans attended the fight, which was held in Cuba. The battle was to go 45 rounds, but by the 26th round, Little Arthur was tired. Willard knocked out the champion with a right uppercut.

Johnson later returned to the United States, where he was jailed for one year. After prison, he moved from job to job, but he never fought again professionally. He became a band leader for a time and then an actor. Later he ran a gym in New York. When he was 68 years old, he was killed in an auto accident.

The 1920s are often called the "Golden Age" of boxing. They were exciting times when some of the best fighters ever to enter the ring battled for the heavyweight title. And one of the most popular and talented of these fighters was Jack Dempsey.

Dempsey became known as the "Manassa Mauler" because he was born in Manassa, Colorado, in 1895. There were 11 children in the Dempsey family, and Jack had to go to work at an early age to help feed the family. He worked at different times as a cowboy, a miner, a dishwasher, and a waiter. Meanwhile, he went to school off and on, finally finishing eighth grade when he was 16 years old.

Dempsey's mother sparked his interest in boxing. She was a great fan of John L. Sullivan and often told stories about the champion to young Jack. Later, Jack got some boxing lessons from an older brother who was an amateur boxer. Dempsey's fighting career began when he left home after finishing school. He moved from town to town, picking up jobs wherever he could. Along the way, he also began to pick up fights, and more important, he won most of them.

By the time Dempsey was 24 years old, he had met and beaten most of the best heavyweights in the United States. There was only one man left for him to face—Jess Willard, the heavyweight champion. The two boxers finally met in Toledo, Ohio, in 1919. Willard was 36 years old, and he had not fought for three years. But most boxing experts still thought that Willard was unbeatable. Up to that time, no fighter had ever been able to knock down the giant champion. In the first round, Dempsey not only knocked down Willard, but he also showed him the floor seven times. At the end of the third round, Willard's corner threw in the towel. Willard had taken enough punches. His jaw was broken, and his cheek was split. Some of his teeth were knocked out, and his nose was flattened.

The new champion then fought a series of bouts that drew the greatest crowds in ring history. One of these was in 1921 against Georges Carpentier, a French boxer. It was the first bout to be broadcast over the radio, and 80,000 people were on hand to watch it in Jersey City, New Jersey. The crowd saw a quick fight. In the second round, Carpentier hit Dempsey on the jaw with a hard blow. Dempsey took it standing, but Carpentier broke his hand on the champ's jaw. The fight ended in the fourth round when Dempsey scored a knockout.

In another big fight Dempsey was matched against Luis Angel Firpo. Firpo was from Argentina, and he had taken 74 straight bouts in South America. More than 85,000 people saw the two heavyweights meet in the ring in 1923. The first round was one of the wildest in boxing history. Only a few moments into the fight, Firpo knocked Dempsey to his knees. When Dempsey got up, he knocked down his big opponent. Then Dempsey stood over Firpo and beat him back to the canvas each time he tried to get up. Firpo fell under the champion's blows seven times.

When Firpo finally got on his feet, he swung a wild right that knocked Dempsey through the ropes. Dempsey fell so hard that he smashed a reporter's typewriter. The fans shoved Dempsey back into the ring just as the bell rang to end the round. The second round ended after 57 seconds. That was all the time Dempsey needed to drop Firpo twice before knocking him out.

Dempsey then went to Europe, where he acted in plays for three years. But boxing fans began to demand that Dempsey defend his title again. Finally, he signed to meet Gene Tunney in Philadelphia in 1926. Tunney had been fighting professionally for seven years. Unlike Dempsey, he did not have a strong punch. Instead, he usually won his matches by tiring out his opponents and then moving in for a knockout.

Jack Dempsey is knocked through the ropes during the first round of his fight with Luis Firpo.

A crowd of 120,000 people were on hand to see what most thought would be an easy Dempsey win. But Tunney's skill won out over Dempsey's strength. Tunney stepped away from Dempsey every time the champion rushed him. But Tunney got close enough to the champ to jab him in the face round after round. By the end of the 10-round fight, both of Dempsey's eyes were swollen shut. Tunney was the unamimous winner in a decision.

After his loss to Tunney, many people thought Dempsey would retire. But Dempsey wanted to try to regain the championship. In 1927, he met Jack Sharkey, a top heavyweight. It was decided that the winner of the match would meet Tunney in a title bout. Dempsey took the fight in a knockout.

Later that year, the second title fight between Dempsey and Tunney was held in Chicago. Almost 105,000 fans gathered to see the match. This time Dempsey knocked down Tunney in the seventh round, and it looked like he had a knockout. But after Tunney fell, Dempsey did not go to the farthest neutral corner immediately as he was supposed to. Because of his delay, the count was not started right away. Tunney made use of the extra few seconds, got up at the count of nine, and went on to win the fight in a decision. Boxing people call this famous fight "The Battle of the Long Count."

After his second loss to Tunney, Dempsey retired from the ring. During World War II, he joined the U.S. Coast Guard as a lieutenant com- mander. He served in the Pacific, where he taught men self-defense. Later he became the owner of a popular restaurant in New York City.

Gene Tunney

Many boxing experts often compare Gene Tunney with Jim Corbett. Like Corbett, Tunney studied the sport very seriously. He always looked for new ways to improve his skill in the ring. Outside of the ring, Tunney was also a "gentleman" like Corbett. He was a quiet man who liked to read in his free time.

Gene Tunney was born in New York City in 1898. One of seven children, Gene quit school when he was 15 years old and went to work. Tunney's family lived in Greenwich Village, a tough neighborhood in New York City. Gene learned how to box because he was tired of being pushed around by neighborhood gangs. Every day after work, he sparred at a gym. Before long, he was fighting boxers all over the city.

Tunney began fighting professionally when he was 19 years old. He was smart, fast, and very calm in the ring. He learned to wear down opponents by dancing away from their wild swings. Then he moved in and hit them when they were tired.

Tunney had fought only a few professional bouts before he joined the Marines during World War I. While Tunney was in the service, he won the light-heavyweight title of the American Expeditionary Force. After this win, he told friends that he was going to go after the heavyweight title when the war was over.

After the war, Tunney kept his word and went after the heavyweight title. But seven years passed before he got a title bout with Jack Dempsey. During that time, Tunney won 29 bouts before taking the world light-heavyweight championship. He lost his first and only professional fight while defending that title. The loss was in a 15-round decision for Harry Greb in New York. But when the two boxers met for a rematch, Tunney took back the title. Tunney then entered the heavyweight class and beat most of the top fighters there. Finally, there was only one man left for him to challenge—Jack Dempsey, the world heavyweight champion.

The Dempsey-Tunney fight was held in Philadelphia in 1926. No one thought that Tunney stood a chance against Dempsey. Sportswriters made fun of Tunney before the bout. They called him the "Greenwich Village Folly." But this nickname was forgotten after the first round. The bell had hardly rung before Tunney fooled the champion by throwing a hard right. The punch surprised Dempsey and caught him on the cheek. Tunney was a smart fighter, and this surprise punch was part of his fight plan. It worked. Dempsey, caught off-guard, was never able to come back. When the 10-round fight ended, Tunney was named the new champion in a decision.

A Dempsey-Tunney rematch was held in Chicago a year later. This was the famous "Battle of the Long Count." Boxing experts still argue about the outcome of this fight. Tunney won the 10-round decision, but not before he was knocked out by Dempsey in the 7th round. Dempsey probably could have had the fight in that round, if he had gone right to the farthest neutral corner after scoring the knockout. But instead of doing this, Dempsey stood over the fallen Tunney for several

The famous "Long Count"—Tunney is on the canvas, but Dempsey has not moved to a neutral corner.

seconds. According to boxing rules, the referee could not start the count until Dempsey went to the corner. By the time he did, Tunney had gotten the extra seconds he needed to recover from the blow. He got to his feet at the count of nine, and from then on, it was all Tunney's fight.

After this match, Tunney fought only one more time. The bout was with an Australian heavy-weight, and Tunney won by a knockout. Tunney then quit the ring—one of only two champions to retire without having lost a heavyweight bout.

Many great boxers became poor men when their fighting days were over. But not Tunney. He was as smart with his money as he was with his boxing skills. Tunney was a millionaire when he retired from the ring. Today he is a successful businessman in New York City.

Joe Louis

When Joe Louis won the world heavyweight title, he promised the fans that he would be a fighting champion. He kept this promise. Louis defended his title 25 times—more times than any other heavyweight ever risked his crown.

Louis was born Joe Louis Barrow in 1914 in Alabama. He dropped his last name after he began fighting professionally. When Joe was 12 years old, he moved to Detroit, Michigan, with his parents and 12 brothers and sisters. Never a good student, Joe quit grade school to learn how to build furniture. At the same time, he began to box every night in a neighborhood gym. From the start, Louis was a very hard hitter.

When he was 18 years old, Louis had his first amateur boxing match. No one watching the bout would have guessed that Louis would become a world heavyweight champion. Louis was knocked down nine times in the first two rounds. But a year after that match, Louis had improved so much that he took the light heavyweight title in the Golden Gloves tournament. And the next year—1934— he won the title again.

In the summer of 1934, Louis moved into the professional ranks. He got off to a good start, winning his first pro fight by a knockout. Then he went on to win 11 more fights that year—9 of them by knockouts. Because of his knockout record, sports-writers began calling him the "Brown Bomber."

One of his first big fights was against Primo Carnera, a former heavyweight champion. Louis took the bigger Carnera in six rounds. He then went on to face Max Baer, another ex-champion. Baer had never been knocked off his feet in the ring—until he met Louis. In fact, Louis knocked down Baer so often that the ex-champ finally got tired of getting up. When Louis knocked him down in the fourth round, Baer just sat there and let the referee count him out. Then, while the ref was raising Louis's arm in victory, Baer got up and walked back to his corner.

There was still another ex-champion left for Louis to face—Max Schmeling, a German heavyweight. Everyone thought that Louis would take the 31-year-old Schmeling easily. But Schmeling had noticed a weakness in Louis's fighting style. After the Brown Bomber jabbed with his left, he then dropped it, leaving himself open for a right punch. Schmeling had a great right-handed punch.

The Schmeling-Louis match was held in 1936 in New York. Louis was winning until he left himself open in the fourth for Schmeling's right punch. After that, it became Schmeling's fight, and Louis was counted out in the 12th round. Louis did not waste any time worrying over this loss. Just a few weeks later, he met Jack Sharkey, another ex-champ who came out of retirement to face Louis. Louis knocked out Sharkey in the third round.

In 1937 Louis finally met the heavyweight champion, Jim Braddock, in a title match in Chicago. Braddock knocked down Louis in the first few seconds of the fight. But Louis got up quickly and never let Braddock drop him again. Braddock's manager wanted to throw in the towel in the seventh round, but the champion wouldn't let him. He wanted to finish the fight in the ring. And that was just what he did. He was knocked out in the eighth by the Brown Bomber.

Louis would never consider himself a real champion until he could fight and beat Max Schmeling —the man who had given him his only professional loss. The German finally agreed to fight Louis in 1938 in New York. More than 70,000 people came to see the match. The fans expected to see Louis start slow and cool in his usual way. But at the opening bell, Louis rushed out and gave Schmeling one blow after another. A hard right to the German's body caused him to scream in pain. He fell down hard. When Schmeling got up, Louis knocked him down again. Then the referee began to count out the German. Schmeling's corner tried to stop

Joe Louis the winner over Billy Conn

the fight by throwing a towel into the ring, but the referee threw the towel back. He then finished counting out Schmeling. For Louis, this was the greatest victory of his career.

In 1941, Louis fought six title bouts. One of these was against Billy Conn, a good, fast boxer. It was the first time that Louis came close to losing his title. Conn had the better of Louis for 12 rounds, but Louis surprised him with a knockout punch in the 13th. That was Louis's last fight for five years. World War II had begun, and Louis quit the ring to join the army. When Louis got out of the service in 1946, he met Billy Conn again in the ring. This time he took care of Conn quickly, dropping him in the 8th round.

The next year the Brown Bomber had a title bout with Jersey Joe Walcott. The 37-year-old Walcott was past his best boxing days. But he was still a smart fighter with a strong punch. Louis, who had not fought for a year, was overweight. Walcott knocked down the champion twice in the first 4 rounds. The tired Louis chased Walcott the rest of the fight, but he could not knock him out. Louis was given the decison, though many fans thought Walcott was the winner. The judges gave the bout to Louis because it is a rule in boxing that a man cannot win the title by running away from the champion. Since Walcott ran away instead of standing and meeting Louis, it was decided that the Brown Bomber was still champ. Louis and Walcott met again in 1948. This time Louis knocked out Walcott in the 11th round. Louis then said he would quit fighting while he was still champion.

But Louis did not stay out of the ring. In 1950, he met Ezzard Charles, the new heavyweight champion, in a title match. The match went a full 15 rounds, with Louis taking a beating. Charles was named the winner in a decision. After this match,

Louis again retired—for one year. In 1951, he went against Rocky Marciano, an up-and-coming heavyweight. Although Marciano was much younger and stronger than Louis, the ex-champ was able to hold him for 7 rounds. But the bout ended quickly in the 8th when Marciano knocked Louis right out of the ring. Louis never tried to come back again after that defeat.

During his long career, Louis earned more than $4 million, but he spent it quickly. A few years after his match with Marciano, he was broke. To earn money, Louis became a professional wrestler for a time. He then began doing public relations work, which turned out to be a successful career for the Brown Bomber.

Rocky Marciano (left) pounds Jersey Joe Walcott during their 13-round bout in 1952.

Not many boxers finished a whole fight with Rocky Marciano. And no one ever beat him in a bout. When Marciano retired from the ring, he had won all of his professional fights—the only heavy-weight champ ever to do so. And Marciano took his opponents by knockouts in 43 of these 49 fights.

Rocky was born Rocco Marchlegiano in Brockton, Massachusetts, in 1923. The oldest of six children, Marciano was a quiet boy who liked to play base-ball. He boxed a little after an uncle gave him some gloves and a punching bag, but he liked being a catcher best. Marciano quit high school after two years and went to work. Then, when World War II began, he joined the army. It was while he was in the army that Marciano began boxing seriously. But though he did well in the ring and even won a title, he never forgot baseball.

When he came back from the war, Marciano got a tryout with the Chicago Cubs. But after a week, he was sent home. Back in Brockton, Marciano worked at a number of jobs until a friend con-vinced him to try boxing again. This time Rocky stuck with it, and he worked his way to the finals of the Golden Gloves tournament.

Marciano had a late start in his professional boxing career. He was 24 years old when he had his first professional fight. That was old for a boxer.

Most fighters are at the tops of their careers by that age. But Marciano did not let his age worry him. In 1948, he went to New York to try to get some more professional bouts. He finally got a tryout match with a big heavyweight.

Marciano and his opponent met in a gym at a boys' club. At first, the people watching the match laughed at Marciano because he had a strange build for a heavyweight. Rocky stood 5 feet, 11 inches tall and weighed 190 pounds. He had powerful shoulders, but his arms were very short for a heavyweight. They were only 67 inches long, almost 12 inches shorter than any other great heavyweight's arms. But the people stopped laughing when Marciano knocked his opponent cold. The short-armed heavyweight packed a very strong punch.

Rocky did not become well known to boxing fans until 1951. That was when he won two big matches. First he fought and knocked out Rex Layne, a good heavyweight. Then he met Joe Louis. Louis had been heavyweight champion while Rocky was growing up. He was a hero to Rocky, and this made it hard for Marciano to fight the ex-champion. For the first 7 rounds, the two fighters seemed evenly matched. But in the 8th round, Marciano hit Louis with a powerful right that

Rocky Marciano shakes hands with ex-champ Joe Louis after signing an agreement for a 10-round bout in 1951.

knocked him through the ropes. It was Marciano's match by a knockout.

In 1952, Marciano met "Jersey Joe" Walcott for the heavyweight title. Walcott had been boxing for 22 years. He had won the title only the year before from Ezzard Charles. In the 1st round, Walcott hit Rocky with a left hook and knocked him down. That was the first time Marciano had ever been floored. By the end of the 12th round, Walcott was leading in points. He just seemed too fast and too smart for Marciano. When the bell sounded in the

13th, Walcott rushed out to jab Marciano. But Marciano got his right in ahead of the champion's left. He gave Walcott a right to the chin, and the champion was counted out. In 1953, the two fighters met for a rematch. This time Rocky knocked out Walcott in the 1st round.

There was only one more top heavyweight for Rocky to meet—Ezzard Charles, the ex-champion. In 1954, Rocky gave Charles two chances to regain the title. Marciano took the first fight, even though Charles stayed with him the full 15 rounds. That was the longest anyone had ever stayed in the ring with Marciano. In their second bout, Marciano took Charles by a knockout in the 8th round.

Marciano (right) uses his powerful right in a bruising battle with Ezzard Charles.

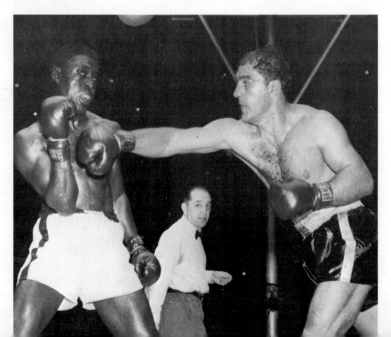

Marciano's last fight was in 1955 against Archie Moore, the light-heavyweight champion of the world. Moore had fought almost 150 bouts, and he had not lost many of them. But he was an aging fighter when he entered the ring against Marciano. To everyone's surprise, Moore knocked down Marciano in the 2nd round. But Marciano was too young and strong to stay down. He got up and went on to knock out Moore in the 9th round.

Marciano then said he would never fight again. And unlike most of the other champions, he never did box again. Marciano retired without ever losing a fight. He earned the name "Brockton Blockbuster" because he scored knockouts in all but six of his fights. After leaving the ring, Marciano became a businessman. He was killed in an airplane crash in 1969, the day before his 46th birthday.

Someone once fed a computer the facts on all the great heavyweights in modern boxing history. The computer picked Marciano as the all-time champion. But some boxing experts do not rate Marciano among the greatest heavyweights of all time. They say he never had to defend his title against any really topnotch heavyweights. That may be true. But it's also true that Marciano beat all the good heavyweights there were at the time he held his title.

Before he even got a chance at the heavyweight title, Muhammad Ali bragged, "I am the greatest!" Many boxing experts did not think Ali was even a good boxer, but, as it turned out, Ali knew what he was talking about. Now, many boxing experts call Ali the greatest heavyweight of all time.

When Ali was born in Louisville, Kentucky, in 1942, he was named Cassius Clay. He later changed his name to Muhammad Ali when he joined the Black Muslim religion.

Ali might not have become a boxer if his bicycle had not been stolen when he was a boy. The bike was taken while 12-year-old Ali watched a basketball game at a neighborhood gym. When Ali looked for a policeman to report the loss, he found one inside the gym, teaching a boxing class. Ali told the officer that he was going to beat up the boy who took his bicycle. The policeman told Ali that he should learn how to box first, and he asked him to join his class. Ali never found his bike, but he did find out that he had a powerful punch.

Four years later, in 1958, Ali won the Louisville Golden Gloves tournament. In 1959, he took both the National Golden Gloves championship and the National Amateur Athletic Union's light-heavyweight championship. Altogether, he won 180 of 184 amateur bouts. Ali's last bout as an amateur was fought in the 1960 Olympics in Rome. There he won the gold medal in the light-heavyweight division.

After his Olympic victory, Ali turned professional. In 1961, his first full year as a pro fighter, Ali had eight bouts. He won six of these by knockouts and took the other two in decisions. It began to look like the 6-foot, 3-inch, 195-pound Ali would go places in the boxing world. But many fans didn't like Ali because he bragged so much about his skill in the ring. He even wrote poems, naming the round in which he would knock out an opponent. And most of the time, Ali scored a knockout in the round he had predicted!

One of the knockouts that Ali predicted was scored in his 1962 bout with Archie Moore, the light-heavyweight champion of the world. Before the fight, Ali said that he would take Moore in four rounds. Ali kept his word. Moore was counted out in round four. The next year Ali went to England, where he met Henry Cooper, the British Empire champion. Ali predicted, "Cooper has to go in five." Cooper did go in five.

In 1964, Ali signed to fight Sonny Liston for the heavyweight title. Ali said he would "float like a butterfly and sting like a bee" in beating Liston. He did just that. Liston's rushes did nothing but get him stinging jabs in the face from the faster Ali. In the third round, Ali opened up a cut on Liston's face. The champ's handlers put medicine on the cut. Some of this medicine got on Ali's gloves when he hit Liston in the fourth round. Then Ali wiped his forehead, and the medicine came off his glove and ran into his eyes.

At the start of the fifth round, Ali said that he was blinded by the medicine. He refused to get out of his corner, and his manager had to push him out. By the end of the round his eyes had cleared, and Ali took control of the fight. Liston could not keep up with the younger Ali, and when the bell rang for the seventh round, Liston stayed in his corner. Ali was named the winner and heavyweight champion by a technical knockout. Liston and Ali met for a rematch in 1965. This time Ali knocked out Liston in the first round.

Ali then went on to beat most of the top heavyweights in the United States and Europe. One of his victims was Floyd Patterson, a former heavyweight champion. Even though Ali could have taken Patterson by a knockout in any round, he made Patterson suffer a 12-round beating. The referee finally stopped the fight and named Ali the winner by a technical knockout.

After the unnecessary beating he gave Patterson,

Ali became very unpopular with the fans. He soon became unpopular with the U.S. Army too. When he was drafted by the army, Ali refused to go on the grounds that it was against the Black Muslim religion to fight in a war. Because of his stand, he was sentenced to five years in prison in 1967. The World Boxing Association (WBA) then took away his boxing license and his title.

The WBA held a tournament to name a new heavyweight champion. The title was won by Jimmy Ellis, an ex-sparring partner of Ali. Mean-

while, the New York State Athletic Commission decided it would also name a new heavyweight champion. The commission said that the winner in a match between two young heavyweights, Joe Frazier and Buster Mathis, would be the new world champion. Frazier, who was nicknamed "Smokin' Joe," won the bout.

While others were fighting in the ring for his title, Ali was fighting in the courts for his freedom. He did not have to go to prison because his lawyers were appealing the case. But Ali was still not free to do what he knew best—box. The WBA would not give him back his license. Finally, Ali announced that he would never fight again.

From 1967 until 1970, there were two world heavyweight champions—Jimmy Ellis and Joe Frazier. They finally met for a bout in New York. Smokin' Joe won by a technical knockout in the fifth round. He was then recognized as the only world heavyweight champion. But Frazier had barely won the title when he received a challenge from an unexpected opponent—Muhammad Ali. The state of Georgia had given Ali a boxing license, and the ex-champ was coming out of retirement. Before he met Frazier, Ali fought and beat Jerry Quarry in Atlanta. New York State then gave Ali a boxing license, and he went there to meet Oscar

Bonavena, an Argentine heavyweight. Ali looked slow against Bonavena, but he scored three knockdowns to win by a technical knockout.

A championship match between Frazier and Ali was held in New York in 1971. The 30-year-old Ali was undefeated in 31 fights. Frazier, at 28 years old, was undefeated in 26 bouts. Because of the two boxers' records, the bout was called "The Fight of the Champions." More than 20,000 people attended the match, and it was shown on TV all over the world. Each of the fighters was to be paid $2.5 million, whether he won or lost.

The fight went the full 15 rounds. As usual, Ali had bragged before the match that he would beat Frazier badly. In the early rounds of the fight, it looked as though Ali's prediction would come true. Ali hit Frazier with one jab after another. Then he danced out of reach when Frazier rushed him. But Frazier never gave up. He kept shaking off the punches and coming after Ali. By the 4th round, Frazier's powerful punches had begun to land. In the 11th round, Smokin' Joe hurt Ali with a solid punch, and in the 15th, he knocked down Ali with a sweeping left hook. Frazier won the bout by a unanimous decision.

Ali was a loser in the ring in 1971, but he was a winner in the courts. After a four-year legal fight,

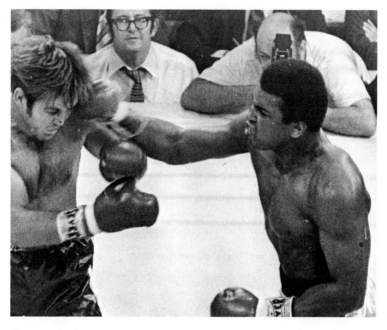

Muhammad Ali lands a hard right to Jerry Quarry's head during their 1970 bout.

Ali won his draft case in a Supreme Court decision. The court said that he did not have to serve in the army because of his religious beliefs.

Many people thought that Ali would retire for good after his loss to Frazier. But instead, Ali kept fighting—and winning. In 1972 Ali met and stopped six fighters. The next year he fought four matches. In one of these bouts, he suffered a broken jaw and a surprising defeat at the hands of Ken Norton, a 28-year-old heavyweight. The fight lasted a full 12 rounds, with Norton winning in a decision. Several months later, the two had a rematch. This time Ali was the winner in a 12-round decision.

In 1974, Ali and Joe Frazier had a rematch in New York. But this time it was not a title fight. Frazier had lost the crown to George Foreman the year before. Ali fought as though the championship was at stake anyway. From the beginning, he took control of the fight. The match lasted 12 rounds, and Ali won it in a unanimous decision.

After beating Frazier, Ali amazed everyone by saying that he was ready to go into the ring with George Foreman to regain the heavyweight title. All the odds were against Ali's winning a fight against Foreman, who was undefeated in 40 fights. Only one other champion—Floyd Patterson—had ever won the heavyweight title twice. But Ali said that he could do it.

He trained for months to get into shape for the fight. Then in October 1974, he met Foreman in the country of Zaire (ZAY-air), in central Africa. Millions of people all over the world watched the bout on closed-circuit television, waiting to see whether Ali could do the impossible. They were not disappointed. Ali was in top condition, and Foreman's fierce punches hardly seemed to hurt him at all. He waited until Foreman wore himself

Muhammad Ali watches as George Foreman is counted out during the eighth round of their championship bout in Zaire.

69

out. Then in the eighth round he delivered the knockout punch that ended the fight. Ali was once again the heavyweight champion of the world.

Muhammad Ali made an amazing comeback after his three-year absence from the ring. And his incredible win over George Foreman leaves no doubt that he will be ranked as one of the greatest heavyweights in the history of boxing.

About the Author

Richard Rainbolt is a longtime sports fan who has
written a number of lively, well-received sports
books. Among them are *Gold Glory*, a history of
the Minnesota Gophers; *The Goldy Shuffle*, the
story of Bill Goldsworthy of the Minnesota North
Stars; and *The Minnesota Vikings*, a fast-paced
history of that famous team. As one might guess
from his books, the author is a native of Minnesota.
After serving in the U.S. Marines, Mr. Rainbolt
attended the University of Minnesota, where he
received a degree in journalism. Since then, he
has worked as a newspaper reporter, a public
relations man, and a reporter for the Associated
Press. In addition to writing, Mr. Rainbolt now runs
his own public relations firm.